# Chirper in Chief

Written by
TINKER BELL

# CHIRPER IN CHIEF

**Tinker Bell**

**Author's Tranquility Press**

MARIETTA, GEORGIA

Copyright © 2021 by Tinker Bell

All rights reserved. No part of this publication may be reproduced, distribut-ed or transmitted in any form or by any means, including photocopying, recording, or other electronic or mechanical methods, without the prior writ-ten permission of the publisher, except in the case of brief quotations em-bodied in critical reviews and certain other noncommercial uses permitted by copyright law. For permission requests, write to the publisher, addressed "Attention: Permissions Coordinator," at the address below.

Tinker Bell/Author's Tranquility Press

2706 Station Club Drive SW

Marietta, GA 30060

www.authorstranquilitypress.com

Publisher's Note: This is a work of fiction. Names, characters, places, and incidents are a product of the author's imagination. Locales and public names are sometimes used for atmospheric purposes. Any resemblance to actual people, living or dead, or to businesses, companies, events, institu-tions, or locales is completely coincidental.

Ordering Information:

Quantity sales. Special discounts are available on quantity purchases by corporations, associations, and others. For details, contact the "Special Sales Department" at the address above.

Chirper in Chief/ Tinker Bell

Paperback: ISBN: 978-1-956480-55-9

Hardcover: ISBN: 978-1-956480-56-6

E-Book: ISBN: 978-1-956480-57-3

**Dedicated to** *Lucy Black and Edna Penrose*

**Inspired by** *K.T. Glow*

*For God hath put in their hearts to fulfil his will, and to agree, and give their kingdom unto the beast, until the words of God shall be fulfilled. (Revelation 17:17)*

Chirper in Chief is a political satire about Trump's presidency. The book briefly depicts Trump making his grand entrance on the political scene. Readers are informed about Trump defeating his political opponents thus becoming the frontrunner of the GOP and later President of the United States of America.

The book also portrays Trump's controversial campaign ties with Russia and his obsession with tweeting. Readers are also enlightened of his disdain for the media.

The illustrations help to bring an imaginative life to the book, especially for anyone who has ever thought of Trump's Mexican wall.

This book was designed for every reader looking forward to a bellyful of laughter.

A long time ago, a great nation was born. They fought to be free from England and won their freedom. Being a new nation, they struggled to find themselves. Every year they grew stronger, and as they grew, they wrote what became known as the Constitution. The founding fathers gave birth to a president named George Washington. The great nation elected senators and congressmen.

Life wasn't always fancy and glamorous. People didn't always see eye to eye, but they were always proud to be Americans. These great men all had flaws, but they still carried a certain eloquence and grace about them. They made America shine with their speeches and actions.

14 | TINKER BELL

Things went great, and everyone wanted to be an American. Every country far and wide heard tales about America, and America set the trend for every nation.

As the world looked up to America and idolized it, a vampire emerged from the underworld. He called himself an outsider. Some people called him the Trumpster. The vampire tested the waters. He knew that xenophobes, homophobes, and religious fanatics walked among us.

The religious fanatics were heaven-minded and believed in no earthly good. To them, all others were doomed pagans. The vampire knew these people hated Obama, so every day he echoed that President Obama had not been born in America. Obama produced his birth certificate, but alas, the vampire sank his fangs even deeper. Perhaps the vampire was a shape-shifter: like a sly old fox, he still led the cry that Obama was a foreigner.

On to his next scheme. He bellowed, "Muslims will be

banned!" His subjects cheered.

That went well, the vampire thought. He pondered and pondered. Then he said, "We will kick the Mexicans out! They are rapists, and even better we will build a wall to keep them out." His followers were even more thrilled.

The vampire felt invincible. One day he bragged that he could shoot someone in public and his subjects would still love him.

Many people knew the vampire was a fraud. They demanded that he release his tax returns. With a sly grin, he snubbed the demand. He decided to just keep preying on the fears of his followers. "I am being audited," he squealed.

Throughout the land millionaires told the public that the vampire's tale was a fib. But each day, the vampire seemed to have his followers more hypnotized. They hailed him a saint! They hailed him a comrade!

One day he proudly sat on a platform and pronounced "Second Corinthians" as "Two Corinthians." His "right- winged" subjects took it for a joke: they thought it was about two Corinthians walking into a bar.

The vampire became the front runner in the GOP race. Everything he accused his opponents of, he was. When he looked in the mirror or stared into water, he saw the ghosts of his opponents staring back at him. He listened to the voices in his head that urged him to keep lying, and eventually the lies became him. Every dawn he strutted like a peacock, vilifying his opponents, and one by one they fell to his bite.

"Low-energy Jeb," he chanted, and Bush disappeared. Yet the vampire had no groove. He could not sit or stand still for an hour without throwing tantrums.

"Look at that face!" he said of Carly Fiorina. It was clear, though, that the vampire's hair and face were a comedian's punchline.

"Little Marco" was the name bestowed on Marco Rubio. The vampire often scoffed at how Little Marco could sweat.

Behold, the vampire had tiny little hands, and when he was set against his most formidable opponent, he sniffed and sniffed and sipped and sipped water as if he had spent ninety days in a desert.

# FATHER OF LIES

"Lying Ted," he named Ted Cruz, his one-time favorite. Yet the vampire was the father of lies. Ted was famous for reading Dr. Seuss and spinning the truth himself. But to Ted's bewilderment, he was no match for the vampire.

It was rumored that after monitoring the vampire's behavior, Satan held an emergency conference. He told his demons he was going on vacation for a while, and that thanks to Putin he knew that the vampire would one day be liar in chief.

Alas, on November 8, 2016, the world was awakened to a daymare. Trump was bestowed the title of leader of the free world and assigned the number 45. Some news anchors cried in disbelief. Others appeared baffled as they spoke.

His mouth was constantly making mischief. Before January 21, he meddled and muddled in foreign affairs. Law and ethics meant nothing to him. He appeared to be in a rush to throw Obama from the White House before Inauguration Day. When Obama put sanctions on his beloved Russia, the fairies watched as Puty laughed. He declared he would "make America great again." To the world's dismay he tried to make America dark again.

On January 21, 2017 the apocalypse of the world began. Heaven cried as it rained in Washington DC. During the vampire's inauguration, somewhere among the VIP members, the fairies knew that the Kremlin's Putin was in disguise. As the vampire took the solemn oath to preserve, protect, and defend the Constitution of the United States, the resistance knew that a Bible meant nothing to the vampire and that his oath was as good as resuscitating a dead bird.

The fairies also read the thoughts of Putin and heard him whisper "Donny Boy, make Russia proud" as he sat there gleaming on Inauguration Day.

He cut funding for the EPA, and he tried to deprive elderly people and pregnant women of health care. He constantly praised Putin and belittled Americans who disagreed with him. He became the first president to have his campaign investigated over ties to Russia. The vampire declared that he and Puty weren't friends. But whenever he spoke about Putin, he spoke like a woman madly in love.

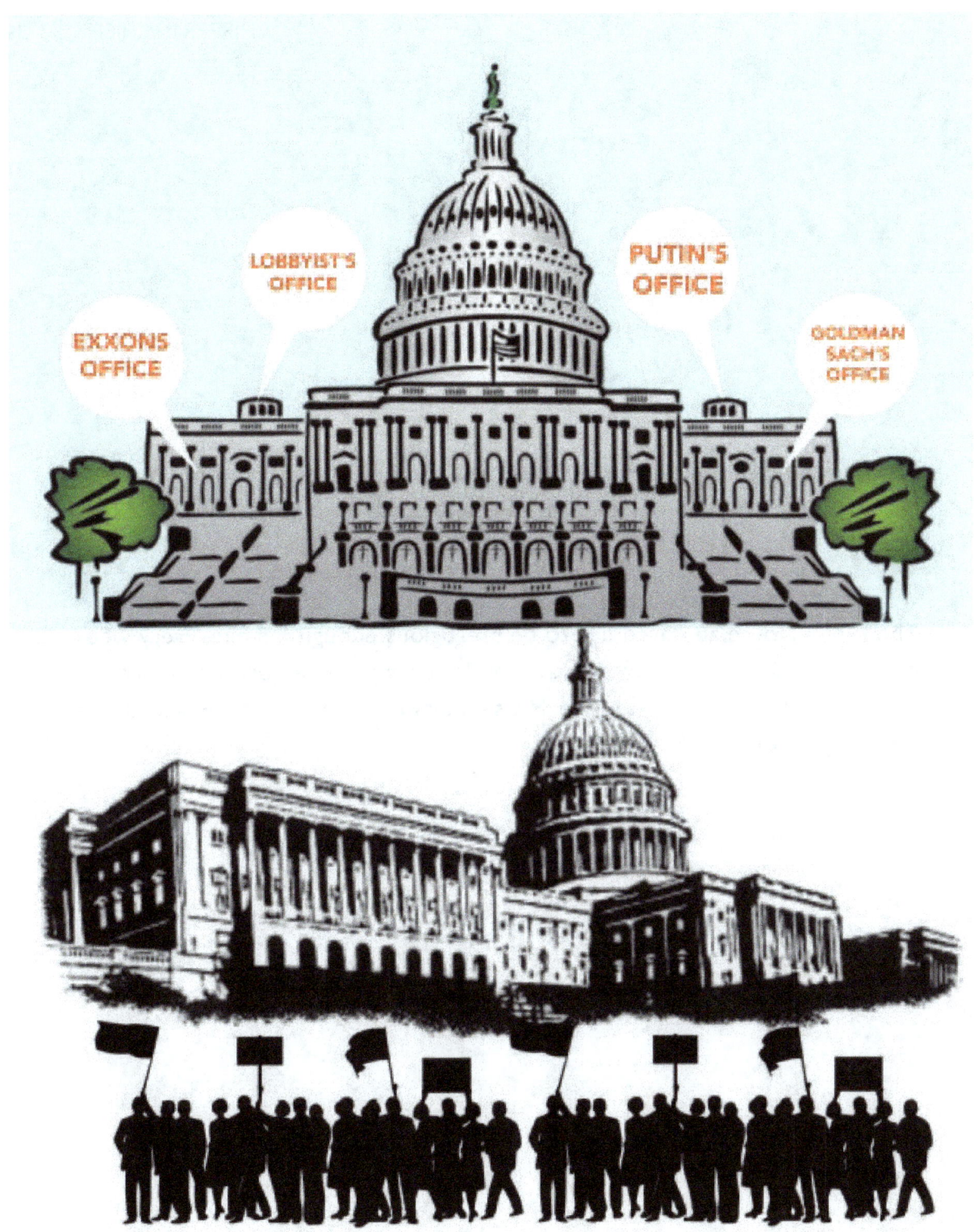

He used the media like a manipulative media whore as they reported his every breath. Later, he lashed out at them and called them fake news, with the exception of his beloved Faux.

The White House appeared not to be prestigious enough for him. Every weekend, he jetted off to his royal palace in Florida, where he golfed and dined on his most delicious chocolate cake. His servants reported that he would also be attending his other palaces.

The vampire told his subjects that he would drain the swamp, yet they journeyed on to Washington with him.

As the vampire ruled, a dark shadow enveloped the White House daily, and the world shuddered and wept for the land of the free and the brave. His rule felt like tremors of the earth, and at times his craziness measured 7 or 8 on the Richter scale. Many people hoped that the vampire's creator would prevent a Trumpetous tsunami.

42 | TINKER BELL

All the so-called patriotic GOP horsemen forgot the meaning of the word patriot. Power, to them, meant party before country, Trump before country. They were revealed as just a bunch of whiners and bullies who had gotten used to lying and manipulating just like their leader. These horsemen were clever, though. Just like the vampire, they had a way to point fingers at the other side.

The vampire ridiculed our generals and bragged that he knew more than them. His patriots, the ones who loved America and wore the flag on their heart every day, turned a blind eye to his follies.

If the nation could find even ten noble, honorable Republicans, a happy nation we would be. But alas, they thumbed their noses at the nation.

As the vampire ruled the land, he often escaped unscathed. He spun theories. Even by his standards, some were low. His translators scurried and scrambled to translate. His servants were at his beck and call to tell the world that, being from another planet, the vampire merely misspoke. One of his councilors, a witch named Kelly Ann, had a meeting and declared

Hear ye, hear ye! From now on,

The White House will call lies Alternative facts.

More and more, it became apparent that the vampire needed many translators. He was constantly sprinkling evil dusts in the air as he polluted the world with his lies and deceit. Albeit, these were now alternative facts.

Not to be outdone was Spicy, the chief's messenger. Day after day Spicy struggled. He was the chief translator for the vampire. His job was very stressful. He chewed gum, he ruffled papers, he yelled at journalists. The words written on the podium from which he spoke were "The White House Daily Fibbing," visible only to the pure of heart. During his daily fibs, a special stand-by unit waited for Spicy: a massage therapist and an ambulance.

Then there were the vampire's sidekicks, like the gremlin Guiliani, who often was seen as the vampire's evil conscience—the one who stood with fork and horns on the vampire's shoulder, cheering him on. Gremlin, who was more articulate, would tell the newsworthy subjects, "Well, you know, remember he is from the Underworld, so he does not speak as well as we do."

Lo, the days moved on and the vampire earned many titles: Toddler in Chief, Dictator in Chief, Golfer in Chief, Coward in Chief, Liar in Chief, and many that even I the writer am ashamed to mention. He cherished these names because he was great at everything he did.

The vampire's favorite toy was a bird named Twitter. The playroom had seven phones with different labels and colors: there was a phone called Sunday Tweet that was red, one colored blue for his Monday tweets, one for Tuesday that was orange, and purple was the color used for Wednesday. He used a green phone for Thursday and a yellow one for Friday. His Saturday phone was brown.

As he explored the rooms of the palace of the White House, he found out about some new toys. He was bored playing with fake toys and told his favorite nanny that he was going to use the real tomahawk and MOAB. In less than two weeks, he bombed Syria and Afghanistan. The vampire felt strong, but as usual he thought that if something went wrong with his new toys, he would blame Obama. He never took responsibility for anything that went wrong, only for things he thought were going great.

As the days drifted along, Spicy realized his job wasn't getting easier. Throughout the land, the subjects argued that he was going to vacate his royal post.

His princess bride remained in Trump Tower. Now and then she peeked outside to see if a handsome prince would come to her rescue. His daughter Ivanka floated around like FLOTUS. Next in line to the throne was not his three sons, but his son-in-law, chief negotiator Jared. Jared and Ivanka were supposed to be the vampire's voice of reason. The fairies revealed the truth to some: that the vampire was devoid of a heart and brain.

Months went by, but they seemed like years. Many of the vampire's subjects became lost sheep. They wandered in the deserts. Some climbed over the Mexican wall, pleading with the Mexicans to return. They begged them to come back and help them with their farms and help them take care of their babies. The Mexicans proudly said no. The Mexicans told them things were going irie in Mexico.

The voices grew even more powerful in the vampire's head. His yes men and lackeys were nowhere in sight. The vampire lost what was left of his mind. He locked himself in Trump Tower and was never seen again.

There will be many tales of the vampire. Forever in the history of mankind, somewhere on a wall in the White House will be a picture of the vampire, the "destroyer in chief," but just above it is a stone engraved with angels spreading their wings, and beneath it a map of beautiful America, inscribed with the following words: "Justice and truth prevailed. God bless America."

I wish to thank God for His daily guidance and love. My thanks to my publisher Author's Tranquility Press for helping me to make this possible.

To my parents, Cecil and Ruthlyn thank you. My darling sisters, Darie Anne, Jodaine and Lakeisha, I can't find the words to express my gratitude.

My lovely daughter Rachel I love you.

Bev, you deserve more than a trip to Jamaica. K.T thank you for our daily talk on Trump and for your positive influence in my life.

Mom/ DR. Murray thank you for being the wind beneath my wings.

Shawn, thank you for being so understanding.

Last but by no means least, to all the fake news channel, thank you for keeping me informed.

As in water face answereth to face, so the heart of man to man. (Proverbs 27:19)

## ABOUT THE AUTHOR

The author is an immigrant from the island of Jamaica West Indies. At an early age, she was an avid reader which surprised her mother, now a retired teacher. She enjoyed sitting with her dad and reading the newspaper and novels he enjoyed reading. In Jamaica, she was also exposed to Pantomime, which was one of the ways the performers would enlighten the public while entertaining them. This inspired her her to to write short stories, poems and skits. Hence her book Chirper in Chief.